# Worship Planning Guidebook

## Lori Broschat

**DISCIPLESHIP** RESOURCES

P O BOX 340003 • NASHVILLE, TN 37203-0003
www.discipleshipresources.org

Cover design by Christa Schoenbrodt.

Interior design by PerfecType, Nashville, TN.

ISBN 13: 978-088177-488-7

ISBN 10: 0-88177-488-X

Library of Congress Control Number: 2006928150

*To those who have taught me to love and
experience worship in many settings:*

*Fellow seminarians and faculty who showed
me how to worship Asbury style!*

*Colleagues and congregations who have been
testing grounds for my material.*

*Those who helped me learn; Cliff, Ross,
Dr. Boyd, and Dr. Kalas.*

*To my family who may not have seen this
coming, but I know they share my joy.*

*And to my dad, who is worshiping at
the throne of grace.*

# Contents

# Foreword

What makes one worship experience vibrate with spiritual depth, and another leave worshipers despairing for an experience of the holy for which they have longed?

How does one worship experience "hang together"–body and soul–thematically, with prayers, sermon, scripture, and hymns all sharing the Good News of a single theme or premise, and another service seem to strike out randomly at a variety of themes, trapping the worshiper in a gigantic pinball machine until he or she finally comes to rest–exhausted, questioning, or dispassionate–at the end of another sacred hour?

Rabbi Abraham Heshchel once said that the holy was comprised of three things: God, a soul, and a moment. When a gifted worship leader weaves scripture, prayers, sermon, entrance, and departure moments into a single whole, then moments are not just moments. They transform into holy moments in which God and souls meet.

We are given new hope for the journey and life takes on richness.

Lori Broshat has provided within the pages of this worship planner a rich treasure trove for those of us who plan for vibrant worship. Within these pages, we will find sound advice for planning worship, for "putting it all together," so that, whether your church worships with 15 or 150, there can be souls "lost in wonder" as worshipers hear the Word and move to do the Word in a hurting world. In short, Lori's work can help you transform mere "moments" into "holy moments" as those under your care meet with God in vibrant worship.

Lori is a practical "prairie wordsmith" whom I appreciate very much. She hails from the heart of the Dakotas prairies and–after a stint for education in the South–began her full-time ministry as the pastor of three churches in North Dakota, two United Methodist churches and one Evangelical Lutheran Church of America. There isn't a prayer in these pages that her congregations haven't prayed, or a suggestion offered that Lori either doesn't regularly utilize in her worship services or teach as part of the Certified Lay Speaking training that she conducts in the Dakotas Conference of The United Methodist Church. She knows intimately well the unique challenges of growing as a disciple of Jesus Christ, as a pastor, and in proclaiming the gospel.

Thank you, Lori, for spending long Dakota winter nights hovering over a computer. You could have been standing in silent witness to the glorious Aurora Borealis! Even more, praise God for the time you have spent with your creator in witness of the early Dakota sunrises, so that these pages might be shared in all of their richness with others.

*Debra Ball-Killbourne*
*Three Rivers District Superintendent*
*Dakotas Conference of The United Methodist Church*

# Introduction

I began life as a Methodist, before there was a United Methodist denomination. For me, church was a part of life, and being active in the church was a lifelong expectation. My parents taught us that being a part of the church meant everyone doing his or her own part. My father served faithfully until his death, my mother continues to serve, and my sisters and their families also share their values. Then there is my story. When I was a small child, worship must not have grabbed my attention too much, because I remember more often than not taking a little nap right there in the pew.

Later, as a teen, I discovered the joy of church music, both vocal and instrumental. I sang in my choir and played my handbells with great enthusiasm and joy. It wasn't until I became a young adult that I truly found my gifts and graces. I was still in the dark at the time as to God's call for my life, but I was fortunate to have a very discerning pastor who saw where I was headed. He offered me opportunities to lead children in music and drama, to teach, to lead small groups, to act, to write, and eventually to preach and lead worship.

Since I have always been fascinated with words, preaching turned out to be easy for me. I discovered quite early the importance of structure within a worship service, the significance of keeping music and scripture in balance. When I entered full-time ministry, I began to take my task of planning worship seriously and intentionally. As I looked for various components of worship liturgy, I was often surprised by what I found and by what I did not find.

Some resources seemed too lofty for the simple Midwestern congregation; others were too urban in their scope. Oftentimes I came up short of any new resources at all. As one accustomed to creating with words, I began to write my own liturgies and prayers, communicating thoughts both direct and humble, as a way of lifting the heart of the worshiper.

I feel very strongly about the purpose of worship being far beyond that of moving from prelude to recessional. When I prepare for worship, I begin by getting a feel for the overall message of the readings. From there I put together the prayers and the liturgies, bringing in key points from the scripture readings and focusing on one main aspect.

Finally, I add the musical selections, taking care to review the words of the hymns and choosing those that complement the liturgy and message.

For me, there is a feeling of disconnect in a worship service where the hymns do not coordinate with the scripture and the liturgy seems random and unrelated. I feel that worship should have a natural flow, an enhancement of emotion that leaves the worshiper feeling that he or she has been spiritually fed, and yet at the same time spiritually challenged. I believe the point of the message itself is best adhered in the heart of one who has been involved in meaningful worship.

When I became involved in training lay speakers, I was once again a bit dismayed at the lack of materials providing worship planning techniques. In speaking to laity, I found that very few had the tools they needed or the knowledge of how to use them. I felt that I could contribute something to all those dedicated servants of God. I want this book to serve the needs of those who are serving congregations large or small. I want them to have a place to go for a fresh idea or a last-minute resource, whether they have five days or five minutes to prepare for worship.

The language of these worship resources is simple and honest. It speaks from the heart of the participant to the heart of God. The planning suggestions are clear and to the point. My hope is that they will be helpful to beginners and pros alike.

Worship is the privilege of being before God in a community of faith. If you bring your heart to worship, the words will follow.

Blessings,

Lori Broschat

# Planning Worship

Congratulations! If you are utilizing this book, then you are in a very special role—the role of worship facilitator. You may be a local or certified lay speaker doing pulpit supply, or perhaps you are a lay leader assisting in your own local church. You might even be the pastor in charge of planning and leading worship. Whatever your responsibility, your role is the same. You are to be a communicator to the people of God in worship, but don't be overwhelmed by that task!

When does worship begin? Is it when we enter the sanctuary? Is it when the singing starts, or at the time of prayer? Worship begins at the moment we think about coming together as the people of God in the house of God. Although worship is not something we do for ourselves, but is instead what we do for God, worship begins with preparation. Planning worship helps to insure that our time spent before God expresses our faith in the fullest way possible.

In our *United Methodist Hymnal* there is a basic pattern of worship found at the very beginning of the book, because first we need to understand the rhythm and flow of worship. Everything we learn after that helps to balance that rhythm and flow. You will find this pattern beginning on page 2 of the *The United Methodist Hymnal* (UMH). There are four components to this pattern that reflect a natural progression of worship. Within these four components there are many ways of rounding out our worship experience. These additional components can be found beginning on page 3 of the UMH.

Note the various options listed on these three pages. No two churches will worship in exactly the same style or manner, even with the basic pattern of worship. According to the size, tradition, and preference of the individual church, the actual order of worship will look very different from church to church. Creativity and personality are to be highly regarded in a worship service, as long as the focus remains on God.

Depending on where the worship service you are planning is to take place, you may add or subtract parts of worship to suit your needs. Below is a sample of a typical Sunday service you may find in a small to medium-sized congregation. I have included several of the components used most frequently in worship in my own parishes. To give you an idea of what these various features may look like, I have included an example of each. Later in this document you will find a collection of various prayers and other liturgical materials to choose from or to start you thinking about how to create a worship service.

The following is an example of a typical Sunday morning bulletin with additional comments added:

## Community Church Anytown, USA

*Our purpose is to praise and worship God and make God's word available to all.*

Fourth Sunday of Pentecost, June 12, 2005

### ENTRANCE

*(First component. Some churches may use subheads for the different areas of focus in each of these four components. The subhead for this component could be* Prepare for Worship.*)*

GATHERING

Prelude

Announcements

GREETING AND HYMN

Call to Worship *(The call to worship may be used to draw out or highlight a scripture text, as in this example from Ephesians 5:1-2. It is typically read responsively)*

Leader: Therefore, be imitators of God,

**People: As beloved children,**

Leader: And walk in love,

**People: Just as Christ also loved you**

Leader: And gave himself up for us,

**People: An offering and a sacrifice to God as a fragrant aroma.**

*(Additional verses may be included depending on your preference. The call to worship may also be an original writing and may take on the nature of an invocation.)*

Leader: Today our joy is complete

**People: Because we are in the house of the Lord.**

Leader: Today, if we hear God's voice

**People: We will take God's words into our hearts.**

Leader: So that where God is, we will be also.

**People: We will assemble in the house of the Lord**

Leader: To praise God's glorious name.

**All: In this, our joy will be made complete.**

Opening Sentence *(The opening sentence can have the same purpose as the call to worship, although it is generally shorter in content.)*

Leader: Therefore, be imitators of God, as beloved children;

**People: And walk in love, just as Christ also loved you and gave himself up for us, an offering and a sacrifice to God as a fragrant aroma.**

*(The opening sentence may also be an original writing.)*

Leader: Praise be to God who calls us from on high!

**People: We come together to praise and worship God in our midst!**

*Hymn: "Come, Holy Ghost, Our Hearts Inspire" (UMH 603)

OPENING PRAYERS AND PRAISE

Invocation: *(The invocation is a prayer acknowledging and requesting God's presence in worship. Often the words of the invocation are not printed, but here is an example.)*

We feel your Spirit moving among us, O God, as we seek to be your people. Enter into our worship time and be present to us through your word and in our prayers and praises to you. Amen.

*Psalter: Psalm 116 (UMH 837)

*Gloria Patri (UMH 71)

## PROCLAMATION AND RESPONSE

*(Second component.)*

*(The subhead for the following section could be* Proclaim the Word*)*

### PRAYER FOR ILLUMINATION

Prayer for Illumination: *This is often a brief prayer asking for God's wisdom and discernment of God's word.*

**Guide our hearts and minds as we hear your word, O Lord, and seek to apply it to our lives. Amen.**

### SCRIPTURE

Old Testament Reading: Genesis 18:1-15

New Testament Reading: Romans 5:1-8

Hymn: "Let Us Plead For Faith Alone" (UMH 385)

*Gospel Reading: Matthew 9:35-10:8

### SERMON

Sermon: "God Proves God's Love"

### RESPONSE TO THE WORD

*This is the point at which a response to the word would*

*occur, according to the worship style of the particular church. This may include an invitation to receive Christ, a service of baptism, or the reciting of one of the creeds of the church.*

(*Additional subhead:* Time of Prayer and Reflection)

Prayer Hymn: "Freely, Freely" (UMH 389)

## CONCERNS AND PRAYERS/CONFESSION, PARDON, AND PEACE

Sharing of Joys and Concerns

Prayer of Confession (*This may be done by the congregation as a whole in recognition of sins and to ask forgiveness of God.*)

**We are an incomplete people, dear God, because we have inherited a sinful nature. We are lacking your perfect will, and we need your presence in our lives to recreate your perfect image in us. Forgive us for those times when we have broken your law. Help us to seek to be obedient people in the world, a world that tries to pull us away from you. Guide us closer to your teachings that we may follow your way. In Jesus' name, we pray. Amen.**

### OR

Unison Prayer (*This may also be done corporately as a means of reconnecting our spirits to God.*)

**Gracious God, we feel compelled to celebrate today in your house! We come together as your people, bound together by your love for us and your saving grace to all humankind. Breathe into us your Spirit. Refresh our souls with your Word. We remember how powerfully you have drawn your people to your side, how your mighty hand has rescued us again and again. Today we celebrate your love in our lives. We praise your Holy name. Amen.**

Silent Prayer

Pastoral Prayer *(This may include prayers of intercession for those mentioned during a time of joys and concerns. It may also be a time to ask for God's blessing and to give thanks.)*

Lord's Prayer *(If not used during communion or at another time.)*

"Threefold Amen" (UMH 898)

*(Additional subhead:* We Bring Our Gifts)

OFFERING

Tithes and Offerings

Offertory

*Doxology (UMH 95)

*Offertory Prayer *(This may be used as a prayer of dedication and thanks for the gifts God has enabled us to give.)*

**We present these gifts, holy God, to your use and service. Multiply and bless them to enlarge their effectiveness to others. In Christ's name we pray. Amen.**

## THANKSGIVING

*(Third Component. In the absence of the pastor, Holy Communion will not likely be celebrated in most cases. However, the congregation may read a prayer of thanksgiving and/or the Lord's Prayer.)*

Prayer of Thanksgiving:

**Eternal God, we feel such overwhelming joy when we are in your presence! You sent your son that we may have life and have it abundantly, and this is where we find ourselves today, living abundantly in your grace. Thank you for your endless mercy and kindness toward us. We continue to live in the promise of your eternal life. Amen.**

## SENDING FORTH

*(Forth Component. The subhead for this component could be Go and Serve.)*

## HYMN OR SONG AND DISMISSAL WITH BLESSING

*Closing Hymn: "Depth of Mercy" (UMH 355)

*Benediction: *The benediction may be pronounced by the worship leader or may be read as a congregation.*

**We have been in the presence of God. How wonderful to be in God's house! We have become the family of God. How joyful to share the love of our brothers and sisters, mothers and fathers! God is indeed good. Amen.**

### OR

Dismissal with Blessing: *This may be used in place of a benediction.*

**May the Lord above grant you peace through your knowledge of God until we are together again in God's house. Amen.**

## GOING FORTH

*Response: "Shalom to You" (UMH 666)

You may have observed that this order of worship differs from the one used in your own church. In some churches, the offering may be taken after the sermon, or there may be no responsive reading of the Psalm. Not all churches include the reading of all four scriptures each week. In some churches the Apostles' Creed or other creeds are used each week.

Compare a bulletin from your own local church and try to identify where each of the four basic components of the worship pattern fall into place. If you familiarize yourself with the progression of worship, then even when you are called on to lead worship in a neighboring church you will be able to put together a meaningful order of worship.

If you are given the task of choosing the music for the service, it is important to select hymns that fit with the theme of the occasion, particularly at seasonal times of the year. If the service uses the Revised Common Lectionary as the basis for preaching, there are lectionary hymns suggested for each reading. These may be found by accessing the website of the General Board of Discipleship at www.gbod.org/worship.

Now that you have closely examined an order of worship broken down into its many parts, I encourage you to become even better acquainted with each of these many facets of the worship service. In the following chapters I will provide further examples of liturgies and prayers. I will also focus more intently on the importance and significance of each element of the worship service for a deeper understanding.

# Liturgies

When we talk about liturgy, we mean the sense of direction the worship service takes. Believe it or not, worship is as much about direction as it is about spontaneity. We plan worship, yet it is not always under our control! We need order to help us focus our worship and to give it a sense of purpose, which can allow us to feel free to praise God in an impromptu manner. Liturgies allow both those who lead worship and those who participate to each have an active voice in the service.

Liturgy has been called the work of the people, our work being what we feel about God individually expressed in a collective voice. Through the liturgy we confirm before God what we believe about God and what we know of ourselves. We stand elbow to elbow with fellow believers and confess our need for preparation to approach God, our trepidation at serving God, and finally our joy at being in the presence of God.

Because liturgies are typically read responsively, the worship leader may act in the role of advocate or priest, who speaks to God on behalf of the people. However, a contemporary understanding of liturgy does not call for the people to remain silent, but rather to answer in language meant to convey their devotion to God. This collective voice may be a response to the nature of the worship, or it may reflect a deep longing to join our hearts with those who have given us our foundation of worship.

You will notice in the liturgies that follow a feeling of reverence, of wonder, of hope, and of great anticipation. These are emotions that God brings out in us, and when we may have trouble articulating them, the liturgy provides a voice. The call to worship may be used to create a more formal opening to the worship service, and given its longer length, it adds dimension and focus to the service. The opening sentence may be shorter yet no less dramatic. However, it is a more succinct method of bringing our thoughts to attention at the start of the worship time.

# Calls to Worship

## 1

L: People of God, rejoice! You have been summoned to the house of the Lord!

P: **We are glad to be here in the presence of our Almighty God.**

L: There is a privilege in being here, both as individuals and as a community.

P: **We recognize our awesome blessings in being the children of God.**

L: What will you bring to this house to show your devotion to God?

P: **We bring our prayers, our presence, our hearts, and our offerings.**

L: People of God, rejoice!

A: **We are in the house of the Lord!**

## 2

L: Blessed are those who follow in the ways of the Lord.

P: **The way of the Lord is a blessing to those who will follow.**

L: Blessed are those who lift their hands and voices in praise to the Lord.

P: **To praise the Lord is a natural reaction for those who love the Lord.**

L: Blessed are those who seek the Lord in every aspect of life.

**P: We cannot help but find the Lord in every corner of our day.**

L: God has blessed those who will obey God's commands and follow God's ways.

**P: May we always be blessed to be faithful to the ways of the Lord.**

## 3

L: Come, let us worship and bow down.

**P: For we are in the presence of God our Creator.**

L: We are here because we have been blessed by God.

**P: We are blessed by God because we are here.**

L: While we are here we are one body.

**P: When we leave here we will be the body of Christ in the world.**

**A: Let us celebrate as the body of Christ, in the house of God, in the power of the Spirit!**

## 4

L: Where the Spirit of the Lord is, there is peace.

**P: We want to find the peace of God for ourselves.**

L: Where the love of God is, there is joy.

**P: We who have the love of God within our hearts are joyful.**

L: Where the people of God come together, there God is in their midst.

**P: We have come together to find that God is here, in each heart and on each face.**

## 5

L: Since you are no longer strangers but members of the community of God,

**P: And having been built up from the ground by the apostles and the prophets,**

L: Fixed together by Christ as the cornerstone holding all people to him.

**P: Therefore we should be joined in spirit as a household of God.**

**A: Let this be a community linked by God, inspired by Christ, and cemented in love.**

Based on Ephesians 2

## 6

L: This earthly home, which we call a body, has an expiration date.

**P: When it is no longer useful to sustain our lives, it will be destroyed.**

L: Until that time we may find ourselves complaining,

**P: Waiting until God is ready to provide us with our new home.**

L: We may feel a little out of place, living in this body until that time,

**P: But oh the wonder that awaits us when God's daring new design is revealed!**

Based on 2 Corinthians 5:1-4

## 7

L: We are not like those who have no hope;

**P: No—for we have trust in Christ who died and rose again.**

L: We know that we will be with God when we die.

**P: And so we declare this message to everyone.**

L: When we hear the call of the angel and the trumpet's blast,

**A: We will be with the Lord forever! Alleluia!**

Based on 1 Thessalonians 4:13-17

## 8

L: Jesus came into the world to save sinners; of this we can be sure.

**P: Christ is interested in saving our souls and changing our hearts.**

L: Therefore, if we who have been shown mercy do not show mercy to others,

**P: Christ will have no reason to demonstrate his patience with us.**

L: Christ has called us to be an example so that others might believe.

**P: Let our lives be spent as an example of those who have been saved from sin in the name of our risen Lord.**

Based on 1 Timothy 1:15-16

## 9

L: If you are able to hear the voice of God today,

**P: Do not shamefully make your hearts impenetrable like stone.**

L: God has seen the rebellion of other generations and other people who would not listen.

**P: God swore anger because of their stubborn ways.**

L: We need to turn our hearts toward God, to open our ears to God's word.

**P: We must share our faith with others to keep them from God's wrath.**

**A: We want to be a part of those who enter the kingdom of heaven.**

Based on Psalm 95:7-11

## 10

L: Before we enter into this place of worship, we must examine our hearts.

**P: They must be free from anger, free from malice, and open to receive God's love.**

L: As we enter into this place of worship, we must prepare our ears.

P: **They must be ready and willing to receive God's word.**

L: While we are in this place of worship, we must utilize our voices.

P: **They must be able to sing and to pray and to communicate with God.**

L: When we leave this place of worship, we must focus our minds.

P: **They must be capable of retaining all the elements of our time spent with God.**

## 11

L: Approaching the throne of God is no light task,

P: **Yet we come boldly, secure in the knowledge that we are welcome.**

L: We have the promise of God that our sins have been forgiven.

P: **The hope that our faith has made us justified.**

L: Thank the Lord for giving us the rights of inheritance as beloved children.

P: **Thank the Lord for believing us worthy of God's extravagant love.**

A: May what we do in life be proof of our gratitude at being taken into the family of God.

## 12

L: How fortunate are those who know the commandments of God and live by them.

P: Without God's direction for life we would not be content.

L: It is more than enough for us to know God, but God also allows us to experience God.

P: All of our lives are an opportunity to seek God and encounter grace.

L: The life that God has given us is a blessing,

P: And the life that is spent living for God is an offering.

A: Obeying, experiencing, and living for God—what a wonderful calling!

## 13

L: Allowing ourselves to be led by the Spirit means first paying attention.

P: **It means tuning in to the voice inside that bears witness to the truth.**

L: Committing ourselves to following Christ means first denying our own nature.

P: **It means putting aside our selfish, rebellious side for the role of disciple.**

L: Preparing ourselves to remain faithful to God means first allowing God in.

P: **It means opening our hearts to reveal where God needs to cleanse us.**

A: **Obedience means less of us and more of the Father, Son, and Holy Spirit.**

## 14

L: Consider how fortunate we are to be included in the body of Christ,

P: **We, who have done nothing to receive grace, have done nothing to deserve mercy.**

L: Consider how much God must care for each of us,

P: **Yet Christ would have died for the sake of just one.**

L: Consider yourselves as the chosen ones of the God of Israel,

**P: Living under the covenant promise made on the cross and sealed by the empty tomb.**

## 15

L: The source of all life beckons us to draw close.

**P: How dare we approach God but with fear and awe?**

L: We need not fear, for God will not harm us.

**P: Though we ought to be mindful of showing God the reverence due to God.**

L: To show our love and respect for God is the closest we can get to repaying God's gift to us.

**P: Along with our love and respect, let us also show God our devotion, our faith, and our trust.**

**A: O God, we can never say thank you enough!**

# Opening Sentences

## 1

Where are your hearts, you who have come to worship God?

**Our hearts are wherever God is. The same is true for our minds and our souls.**

## 2

The Lord loves those who follow the Lord's teachings and obey the Lord's commandments.

**How long we have been waiting to show our obedience and our love to God!**

## 3

Our lives are intertwined as a family of faith and a body of believers.

**We will celebrate this great relationship as we join together in sharing this space in worship to God.**

## 4

The Spirit of God is alive inside each of us, spurring us on toward the end of our journey.

**By the grace of God we will run this race until we reach that Promised Land.**

## 5

When we enter into the house of the Lord, we know that here we will be of like mind and spirit.

**Let us then show our sense of unity to God and to each other so that when we leave here the world will see in us the Spirit of God.**

## 6

God has made for us a home far beyond these earthly bodies and structures made by human hands.

**Now it is only a matter of time before we will be taken to our glorious home; for the time being we must wait and worship.**

## 7

We are here today, joining our voices with the entire body of Christ in celebration of our joy.

**Our joy comes from our relationship with Christ and the knowledge that we are not left to save ourselves from sin.**

## 8

If we think of ourselves as being in the presence of God, then we will begin to understand a bit of who God is.

**What it will take for us to really know God is to keep focusing on God and learning from God.**

## 9

We know the great and glorious God in many ways.

**Worship is only one of the ways we can show ourselves to God. May our lives be spent learning all the other ways to show God how much we care.**

## 10

When we are together in the name of Christ, we are like sheep gathered into the arms of our shepherd.

**The safety we know in Christ's wondrous arms is the only thing that makes us certain we are loved unconditionally.**

## 11

God is why we are here today to give thanks, to praise, and to worship.

**Each of us in our own way responds to God for the many ways God's love is shown to us.**

## 12

Of all the ways we relate to others, it is how we relate to God that reveals who we truly are.

**There is no room for putting on airs or trying to impress in our relationship with God. God knows what we are inside and how much potential we have.**

## 13

Because we hope in what we cannot see and put our faith in what we have been promised,

**We look to God for guidance and grace to live and work and love and worship as obediently as we can.**

## 14

Can you feel the Spirit's presence among this body of believers?

**It causes our hearts to stir, our minds to create, and our voices to rise in joyful praise and celebration.**

## 15

Awaken your souls now if you are true to the one God of all nations and all people.

**How can we help but shout with joy when we feel the love of God joining our hearts together and making us into a community of believers?**

# Litany of Discipleship

From the beginning when your Spirit swept across the deep and chaos reigned,

**You have been our God.**

Since you have called on men and women of old to bring your light to the world,

**You have been our God.**

From the time when the hardened hearts of your people caused you to make the greatest sacrifice,

**You have been our God.**

Since the day the earth shook and trembled as the seal over the tomb was broken,

**You have been our God.**

From the moment that your Son bid farewell to the disciples and entrusted them with the kingdom of God,

**You have been our God.**

Until that glorious day when the trumpet sounds and the skies roll away, revealing Christ in all his glory,

**You shall be our God.**

When at last heaven and earth are returned to the splendor of that beautiful Eden and we are safe at home,

**You will forever be our God.**

# Litany of Thanksgiving

When we feel your healing touch upon our bodies.

**Our gratefulness belongs to you, O God.**

When we see your face on the faces of others.

**Our gratefulness belongs to you, O God.**

When your splendid Word touches our hearts.

**Our gratefulness belongs to you, O God.**

When love sweeps over us because we have shown love.

**Our gratefulness belongs to you, O God.**

When our faith holds us together as life tears us apart.

**Our gratefulness belongs to you, O God.**

When we know the joy of forgiveness.

**Our gratefulness belongs to you, O God.**

When we know that Christ is ours.

**Our gratefulness belongs to you, O God.**

When the Spirit speaks to us in prayer.

**Our gratefulness belongs to you, O God.**

When the day is done and we are safe in your arms.

**Our gratefulness belongs to you, O God.**

When at last we close our eyes in eternal rest.

**Our soul belongs to you, O God.**

# Litany of Praise

Above the earth lie the heavens.

**God created heaven and earth.**

Within the heavens reside the saints.

**Christ saved the saints from sin and death.**

Out of the heavens the Spirit speaks.

**The Holy Spirit gives us the words of truth.**

Below the heavens lies the earth.

**We do not belong to this earth forever.**

Upon the earth reside believers and nonbelievers alike.

**Christ still calls to those who will hear.**

From the earth we lift our voices in prayer and praise.

**The Spirit prompts our words and carries them upward.**

When earth is no more, heaven will be our home.

**Then we shall see these three, Father, Son, and Holy Spirit.**

# Prayers

At the heart of prayer is a longing to be heard. We know, of course, that with all forms of communication our goal is to be heard and hopefully understood, but in interpersonal communication we don't always make ourselves clear. Often we are speaking for effect or even to catch the ears of those around us. We exaggerate or embellish our thoughts to impress because along with being heard, we also want to be liked and admired.

When it comes to prayer, we are not out to impress, but to genuinely express our true feelings to the Father, the Son, and the Holy Spirit. Now, when we pray privately in our own personal space, it is our voice we use. In worship we may be speaking in groups of dozens, hundreds, or even thousands, yet we still want to capture that same feeling of intimacy. As worship leaders, we traditionally direct corporate prayer, and so it is key to remember to speak using corporate, plural terms such as "we" and "our" and "us."

Prayer may be confessional in nature, which is an important element in our relationship with God. Through the use of a prayer of confession we come before God on our knees, symbolically if not literally. Unison prayers also offer a chance to demonstrate our sense of reverence to God, although in a slightly more joyful manner. Quite often the theme of the service based on the scripture, the music, and other components can determine the use of confessional over unison prayer. Bear in mind that the worship leader alone may pray prayers of confession, or they may be prayed in unison.

At various times in the worship service prayer becomes a response, a preparation, or a transition. A prayer for illumination is a way of preparing our hearts to receive God's written word. The invocation is actually something of a salutation or a calling out to the persons of the Trinity to bless our worship.

As I mentioned earlier, the longer prayer may be confessional to reflect our repentant hearts, or simply an acknowledgement of God in our lives. This may precede a time of silent prayer or pastoral prayer that incorporates the prayer requests of the congregation. Of course, including the Lord's Prayer in unison is a wonderful way to conclude. At the time of the offering, a prayer of dedication may be used either before or after the collection as a way of blessing our gifts.

While we may hesitate a bit to utilize written prayers to speak on behalf of the assembled body of believers, we should not fear. Not everyone is comfortable with praying extemporaneously or spontaneously, and so written prayers are a method of joining our voices in a purposeful way. Wherever and however you choose to integrate prayer within the worship service, pay attention to the theme, which is generally directed by the scripture being taught or perhaps the particular season in the church year. Be sure to be equitable in your means of addressing your prayers among the persons of the Trinity.

# Invocations

## 1

We feel you moving among us, O Lord, as the Spirit quickens our hearts. We want to absorb as much of your presence as possible to become complete. Show us your mighty power, your endless love, and your infinite mercy. We will celebrate and sing because you have called us here. In your name we pray. Amen.

## 2

We are gathered today because this is God's house, and we are God's children. Where else would a family be together but in the home of their Father? We do not have to search for God, for God is always here with us. God anxiously awaits our arrival, and welcomes us with open arms. Now let us celebrate this great family reunion! Praise God!

### 3

Inspire us again, living God, to stand together in your presence and show our devotion. We are very fortunate to be a part of this group today. Help us to see you on each face, to feel you in each embrace, and to share your love with everyone we meet when we leave this place. Amen.

### 4

Amazing Creator and Sustainer, we are so blessed to be the recipients of your love! We cannot help but shout for joy when we come together to worship you! Let not our tongues be silent nor our hearts empty of praise throughout this service. It is to you and for you that we raise our voices in song and prayer. Receive our humble words. Amen.

### 5

Of all the places we could be today, almighty God, we have chosen to be in your house because we love you. We look for you in nature, we speak to you in prayer, and we worship you in community. While we are here we set our sights on being attentive to you. Speak to us in ways that will draw us ever closer to you. Amen.

## 6

Allow us to say how anxious we are, gracious God, to be together with you and our brothers and sisters in faith. Your love calls us here to learn, to share, and to contemplate how we can be better Christians. We ask you to enlighten us as we worship, and help us to be as close to perfect as we can on this side of heaven. In Christ's name we pray. Amen.

## 7

Here we are, Lord Jesus, together in one place to worship. We represent your body, called from across the globe, assembled into a wealth of spiritual gifts and graces. We anxiously await what you have to teach us today. Open our ears and our hearts so that we may know more of you. Our attention is fixed on you, our Savior. Amen.

## 8

For this moment, eternal God, we are yours exclusively. There is no outside noise competing for our attention.

There is no need to outdo or impress each other. We have one purpose only—to worship you. So share with us what you want us to be, where you want us to go, what you want us to do. For this moment, eternal God, we are yours exclusively. Amen.

## 9

What a blessing to be in the place where the Holy Spirit calls us to be in community. We know, of course, that we are continually in community, but it is here alone that we feel connected. Here we seek the face of Christ and the love of God through prayer and praise. Awaken our senses to acquire what we seek! Amen.

## 10

Our desire to be here, loving God, is all due to your prompting of our hearts. On our own we are unreliable in our faith. We tend to lapse in our discipline and our obedience. So it is to this house you have brought us, that our feet may be placed once again on the right road. We are ready to be directed by you, holy God. Amen.

# Prayers for Illumination

## 1

When the scriptures are read, dear God, it is your voice we hear. Fill our hearts with your meaning and truth, so that we may live out what we learn. Amen.

## 2

Loving God, you have provided the words of life. Open now our minds and hearts to receive new life through the reading of your word. In your mercy, Amen.

## 3

We are waiting, everlasting God, for the wisdom that you alone can give. As you inspired those who composed for you, so inspire those who listen. Together we will take your word to the world. Amen.

## 4

Great God of the ages, free us from ignorance and judgment as we come to receive your instruction. Make of our hearts a clean slate for you to once again write upon.

Show us your will through your words. In the name of Christ. Amen.

## 5

Prepare us, almighty God, to become closer to you through scripture. Let these words become our link to the past and the future of your Church. Help us to hear them as you intended them to be. Amen.

## 6

There is a sense of anticipation among us, O God, when we hear the lessons of your book. We expect to be touched, we expect to be changed, and we expect to be inspired. You expect us to respond. May we both get what we expect! Amen.

## 7

We love your lessons of life, God of all nations, for the knowledge they give. We know you are true to your word, Lord. Make us true to that word, as well. May Christ make it so. Amen.

## 8

Awesome God, your voice travels through history along the lines of your holy book. We know you are speaking to us just as you spoke to those who penned these verses. May we be as willing to listen. In your name we pray. Amen.

## 9

Your word comes to us in so many ways, O Lord. You speak to us in music, in nature, and in prayer. Now speak to us through Scripture in words we can take to heart and live out. Amen.

## 10

Why do we take so long to gain understanding, dear God? Why are we so consumed by our own thoughts that your word becomes lost? We know that it is due to our failure to listen. Prepare us now as we open ourselves up to receive the words of life. Amen.

## 11

Coming to the experience of your teaching, glorious Lord, is a powerful moment for us. We approach your word with great respect and anticipation, for we know that these are lessons for life. Give us the ability to hear and to understand, as well as to listen and believe. In Christ's name. Amen.

## 12

We are often blinded, dear God, by the business of the world and the cynicism of those around us. We forget that you have the words of life and have spoken them to us already. Help us now to receive a new word of truth to dispel those rumors of the world. Amen.

# Prayers of Confession

## 1

It is amazing to us, O God, how much time we let go by without opening our hearts to you. We tend to rush through life, always intending to make a point of worship, to make time for prayer. All too often the time slips away until we find ourselves at Sunday again. Forgive us for neglecting our relationship with you. When we are forgetful, gently remind us. When we are less than attentive, restore our focus. Help us to reclaim our faith as the most important element of our lives. We worship at your feet even when we are not in church. In your glory, we pray. Amen.

## 2

Holy God, we come to you in search of mercy. We know that as we approach your throne we are meant to be humble, yet bold. We must be humble due to our need for forgiveness, but we may be bold because we have been forgiven. Our lives reflect this search for mercy as each day we turn our hearts to you. Now as we worship together, let us turn our hearts to each other in Christian community. Together we bring you the praise that you deserve. In Christ our Lord. Amen.

## 3

Many times, loving God, we fail to keep our word. We make promises to family, to friends, to ourselves, and to you. When the day comes to a close and we look back, how often we are disappointed in ourselves. How often, Lord, are you disappointed in us? When you, who are always faithful, always true, look at us, what do you see? We may see ourselves as reliable and dependable, but the truth is that without you we are only human. You give us our strength and our ability, and for that we give you thanks. We praise your holy name! Amen.

## 4

Our hearts are yours, sovereign Lord. Before you we lay ourselves completely open, asking for your hand to make your mark on our souls. When we are left to our own devices, we don't always make the best choices. With your hand upon us, we will be much better suited to live Christian lives. May we always remember the great gift you gave to make us free—free to choose life over death, salvation over sin. You have saved us from ourselves. Praise be! Amen.

## 5

Blessed Savior, we come to you asking that you forgive us of our trespasses. Soon we will be called to forgive those who have trespassed against us. Without your forgiveness we will have nothing to offer to anyone else. We need to be reminded, Lord, of what you have done for us that gives us the boldness to come before you. It was your great love for us that gave us the freedom to believe that our sin can no longer hold us hostage. It was your blood that healed our wounds. Now let it be our faith that keeps us believing in the effectiveness of what you have done. We are humbled to think that it was all for us. We praise you. Amen.

## 6

By your word, most holy God, we know that we do not end with this world. You have promised us that we will dwell in your house forever. In this life, we must walk by faith, but in the next life your saints are walking by sight. We long to know what they know, to witness the splendor of being in your presence. For now, we wait, a bit impatiently, for the day when we will see you face to face. Guide our steps to keep us moving in the right direction, on the path that leads to you. Through the testimony of the faithful we will remain faithful in hope. In the glorious name of Christ. Amen.

## 7

We are an incomplete people, dear God, because we have inherited a sinful nature. We are lacking your perfect will and we need your presence in our lives to recreate your perfect image in us. Forgive us for those times when we have broken your law. Help us to seek to be obedient people in the world, a world that tries to pull us away from you. Guide us closer to your teachings that we may follow your way. In Jesus' name we pray. Amen.

## 8

We try so valiantly, dearest Lord, to be found worthy of what you have given to us, but we fail in our attempts. We fail to realize that we cannot earn our salvation, we fail to live out our faith fully, and we fail to look at others through the eyes of Christ. Forgive us for these failures and for others and bring us to a new realization of the wondrous grace that has been bestowed on us. Without grace, we have no hope. Continue to bless us even as we struggle and fall through life. Amen.

## 9

A mere passing moment, gracious God, is the human life in your eyes. We place so much value on time and accomplishments, and yet there is nothing we do that will ever compare to what you have done for us. In this knowledge we are somewhat humbled and perplexed. We like to be in control, we like to achieve and build and provide. Show us where we need to step back and let you take over. Then our lives will reflect our dependence rather than our pride. Through Christ make it so. Amen.

## 10

Magnificent Spirit, lead us now into a realization that we are bowing before the maker of the universe, and that we are loved. We never feel quite able to be ourselves in God's presence, nor do we feel permitted to put on airs. We are at a crossroads of emotion and fear because the mercy and love of God are so great. Now we ask for your direction of our words, our thoughts, and our prayers so that God will be pleased with our presence. We are so pleased to be in the presence of God! Alleluia! Amen.

# Offertory Prayers

## 1

Great God on high, you have blessed us in so many ways. We cannot begin to express our gratefulness, but these gifts are a beginning. May those who are touched by them be as blessed as we who have been touched by you. Amen.

## 2

Our gracious God, how can we show our appreciation to you for the many ways you have enriched our lives? When we look at what you have done for us, we are unsure how to adequately respond. By our faithful giving, we hope to give back to you a portion of our blessings. In Christ's name. Amen.

## 3

Loving God, your love to us is so great that at times we are overwhelmed. We recognize our reliance on you, as well as the need to share what we have with others. Take these offerings and use them to make a difference in the world, so that all may know you. Amen.

## 4

Forgive us, O Lord, for our lack of understanding of how richly we are blessed. On our own we would be hard pressed to care for ourselves. We need your mercy and your blessing all of our lives. As we give, therefore, it is in response to what we have been given. We ask your blessing on these gifts. Amen.

## 5

Life is good, merciful God, and we know that it is all because of you. You are the one who provides us with all we need. Let our lives reflect this realization of truth, especially when we give to your church. It is here that our gifts are laid down expressly for your kingdom. Bless them, O Lord. Amen.

## 6

How do we say thank you, loving God, to all your many kindnesses to us? We know what is required of us—to walk by faith, to love others, and to give as we are able. Help us to do all three to the best of our ability. These offerings represent our desire to please you through obedience. May it be so. Amen.

## 7

Creator God, who lives and reigns on high, we place these humble offerings on your altar. Where they go from this place is in your hands. Whomever they touch is unknown to us. Bless the work that they will do in this world. Amen.

## 8

Part of our being true to you, Dear Lord, is trusting our resources, our finances to you. Help us to be true through our giving and our service. May those who came before us lead our way. Amen.

## 9

We present these gifts, holy God, to your use and service. Multiply and bless them to enlarge their effectiveness to others. In Christ's name, we pray. Amen.

## 10

O Mighty One who established heaven and earth for our sake, we have brought these gifts for your use. In your kingdom let them exceed the work that we can do alone. Together with other faithful disciples, we entrust our lives to you. In your holy name. Amen.

# Unison Prayers

## 1

This time together is a sustaining moment, heavenly Father. It is an interjection of peace in the midst of our hectic lives. How we long to come into your house as a family of believers. It is here that we find a common ground that is missing in the world around us. Here is where we sing, where we pray, where our hearts become filled with the presence of your Spirit. Here is where we know that we are disciples from the lessons we learn. We go from this place to live out the joy we have experienced. Help us to be true to all that we believe about you. Amen.

## 2

Lord of all the earth, what a wonderful day you have given us today! Every time we come together to celebrate your love in our lives is a wonderful day. We count our blessings as we recall the many moments of our lives spent in worship. In your house we have felt loved, connected, inspired, and Spirit filled. Because you have called us here, we come in obedient faith to join our voices with the saints of the past. We are reminded of the glorious day when we will gather with them around your throne. As we await the day, we pray in the name of Christ. Amen.

## 3

Where can we go, almighty God, that you cannot be found? We tend to think of the church as the house of God, but the church exists within each of us. It is not limited to where God's people are together, but it is expressed in the world through our voices. While we are here, we are of one mind, one purpose, but never let us forget how we have been called as disciples. We must go back out into the world and show our fellow human beings the face of Christ. In our community and beyond, make us shine with your light. In the name of Jesus, we pray. Amen.

## 4

Amazing God, we stand in awe of your presence, at being invited personally to be a part of your family. When we come together in worship, we are joining with those early followers who met in their homes. We have the same spirit of excitement, of newness that those first believers had. However, we have the richness of the church and the history of our faith in words, music, and prayer. Help us to combine these elements into an amazing worship experience. In your grace, we pray. Amen.

## 5

Never let us forget, O Lord our God, how closely tied we are to each other through our relationship with you. It is easy for us to let go of our sense of community or to treat it with casualness. Coming together means more than gathering for worship. It means being of like mind for the sake of Christ. In Christ we share a common bond, a union unlike any other on earth. You have ordained this relationship and have given the body of faith your distinct instructions. Help us to be obedient to your word. Amen.

## 6

Our most holy God, how we have waited to be here! Each time we come to worship, we leave a bit of ourselves behind, and we take a bit of you with us. Worship is a strengthening exercise, a workout for our faith. Make us ever conscious of our spiritual health. Feed us with your Word, strengthen our knees in prayer, and grant us your gentle rest. Show us where we need to improve our hearts and minds, where we must trim the sin from our lives, and build up our muscles of faith. Help us to be true "cross trainers" who continue to run the race. We pray it in Jesus' name. Amen.

## 7

It is incredible to us, great God of heaven, that you have given your endless love to us; that you have offered us eternal life. What have we done to deserve this? What can we do to repay you? The answer is nothing and nothing. We have done nothing and we can do nothing, yet we stand in your glory. We praise you, God, for the kindness you bestow that we can never duplicate. We ask for your grace to help us grow into faithful and loving people in your name. Your own faithfulness and love are incredible. We are blessed! Amen.

## 8

"Where is God?" the world may ask. We would answer, "The better question would be, 'Where is God not?'" We who have eyes to see and ears to hear find you everywhere. We seek you everywhere, and we want to find you everywhere. We want you on our lips, on our minds, and in our hearts. We want to be so filled with you that the

WORSHIP PLANNING GUIDEBOOK

world sees you through us. We want to speak with God's words, to feel with God's compassion, and to touch with God's hands. Most of all, we want to know God's embrace. How marvelous to know God loves us! Hallelujah! Amen.

## 9

O Great Shepherd of the sheep, fill us with your presence now. We feel close to you on our own, but in this place we feel even closer because where two or three are gathered, there you are. We love to be in worship, not only for you, but also with you. This is why you have made us, why you have made your sacrifice for us. You have provided us with a shepherd, we who were without hope or direction. You have brought us to this place of green pastures and still waters, to where goodness and mercy are all around us. We look forward to your anointing and protection for when we must depart. In the name of Christ our Lord. Amen.

## 10

Father in heaven, accept our prayer this day as we come together as a body of faith. Forgive us for those times when we have offended others by our words or actions. Show us where we need to focus our attention and our energy. Bless the work that we do. Bless the way we conduct our lives and guide us into the path that leads to a righteous life. Monitor our hearts and minds to keep us on that path throughout our lives. We look to you for all that we have and all that we do. Live in us and fill our hearts with your love. Amen.

## 11

God who gives us life and liberty, we thank you for your great mercy to us as your children. Help us now to extend that same mercy to our fellow human beings. After the example of Christ, your Son who gave himself up for us, make us true servants rather than those who must be served. Show us where we are at fault, where our pride has become our obstacle, where we have neglected others. Make our words your words, our hearts your hearts, and our lives will be an offering to you. As Christ has shown us humility, may we show humility to the world. In the matchless name of Jesus. Amen.

## 12

Amazing and complicated Creator, how we long to know all that we can about you. We look for knowledge in what the world offers us and we are often disappointed. The wisdom of the human race cannot match the wisdom of God. So we ask that you prepare our minds to listen and learn, as well as preparing our hearts to receive and to give love. From our viewpoint you are quite a mystery, yet the greatest mystery remains how you have saved us from death. What a gift we have been blessed to receive through no effort of our own! We are fully aware of how much we need you and how much more we have to discover. Bless us in our search, O God. Amen.

# Sermon Preparation

If there is anything I have learned about sermon preparation, it is to expect the unexpected. That statement applies to all the elements that make up a sermon, as well as anticipating interruptions in the process. The truth is that where a sermon takes you is not always the direction in which you set out. Preparing a sermon is a detailed and disciplined task, yet one that should always have the flexibility to allow God to intervene and direct us where God wants us to go.

The best and most likely place to begin preparing a sermon is by choosing a text. Whether taken from a weekly lectionary reading or simply a scripture passage of one's own choosing, the text is the heart of the message. There may be times when the message will be on a particular topic, and so with that in mind a text may be chosen to complement that topic. Scripture, however, should never be chosen to fit into our own wishes and desires for communication. Scripture must have the first and last word.

The methods employed by preachers to construct sermons vary from person to person. My personal preference is to begin from the point of scripture. Whether I am working from one passage or four as per the lectionary readings, I begin by examining and reexamining the text from different angles. I look at how a passage stands on its own and how it relates to others. I read a variety of translations to clarify a particular verb or phrase.

This reading and rereading may take place over the course of one day or perhaps two days, but my goal is to let the words sink in and become a part of my thought process. From that point I begin to do the work of exegesis, or drawing out from the text the main point or idea that I feel God is communicating to me. I make initial notes to serve as my own interpretation and help me to develop the flow of the message. I then may begin to look for accompanying illustrations or quotes to bring a personal application to the message.

When it comes to the point of assembling and composing the sermon, I often find that my casual outline form may become revised as I proceed. Here is where the unexpected often takes place. Either while working with the text, or as a natural development of thoughts progress on paper, I may find the sermon taking a slight turn.

Perhaps I initially planned to focus on a particular verse, but in the writing process another point comes into focus.

It is difficult to explain how God works through this process, but for me it has the feeling of a silent communication. I find new enlightenment in places that I had not seen clearly before, or a theme may start to develop that ultimately changes the direction the sermon takes. As long as I have not completely missed the mark on which I began, I know I am okay. I leave the editing up to God.

Sermon titles present an interesting task as to when and how to create them. It is my belief that the sermon title should be the point of the sermon summed up in a few words; however, expressed in a way that does not give the sermon away. The title should arouse curiosity and make the listener want to know what is ahead. I was taught in seminary that choosing the title prior to writing the sermon is perfectly acceptable, as long as the finished product coincides with the title. I like to use a little humor or play on words, but in a subtle way.

Probably the two most difficult parts of the sermon to write are the introduction and the closing. The introduction should gain the attention of the listeners and also provide a smooth transition into the body of the message. This may involve a humorous story or a personal anecdote, or in the case of a more topical sermon, a retelling of a recent news event.

Directly after the introduction the theme of the sermon should be established, ideally by addressing the scripture text. I prefer to provide an interpretation of the text and then follow up with an appropriate, brief illustration. My own rule of thumb is to use no more than two illustrations in a message and to concentrate most of the material on the scripture itself.

Bringing the sermon to a conclusion takes work, particularly in recognizing where a natural conclusion should take place. The length of a sermon depends on the preference of the speaker, but knowing when to end is important. Preferably the sermon would come back to its initial point while offering a bit of a challenge to the listeners. They should be left with something to think about and apply to their own lives.

As I said earlier, what works for one preacher might not work for another, so there is no right or wrong way to prepare a sermon. There is, however, a need to let inspiration work through you so that the message becomes what God intended it to be. I find that when I can get out of the way, when I eliminate my own biases or difficulties with a text, those are the sermons that become the most rewarding to deliver and the biggest blessings to my listeners.

# Sermon Starters

The sermon starters in this chapter represent an assortment of sermons that I have preached in the rural setting of my ministry. Some involve only one text; others make reference to two or more. I offer them as a resource for those looking for ideas, and as a reference point for those who are fairly new to the process of sermon preparation. My hope is that they will inspire you to approach the preaching role with the joy and anticipation that produces a meaningful sermon.

## The Foolishness of God
## Matthew 5:1-12, 1 Corinthians 1:18-31

We do not like the idea of being foolish. We would rather people thought of us as brilliant. But when you are a fool for God, it is not an insult. God wants us to buy into a brand of wisdom that is foolishness to the world. Paul presented the evidence that quickly convicts us as fools—the cross. He said that the cross, that symbol on which we literally hang our faith, is a message of sheer absurdity and folly to those who cannot buy its truth. That makes fools out of those of us who believe the truth.

The cross is what God wants us to take pride in. In fact, it is the only thing in which we are allowed to boast, because the only part we played in the cross was putting

Jesus there. The world has always had a problem with the cross. For the Jews, Messiah was power, victory, and the rise of the nation of Israel. Crucifixion meant weakness, defeat, and unspeakable humiliation. These two ideas did not go together. They did not mesh with the kind of Messiah they wanted or expected.

Yes, God may have been at a weakest and most foolish point on that cross, at least in the world's eyes. This foolishness that God demonstrated was only at the top of a long list of foolish acts. It is foolish to expect a great body of water to separate. It is foolish to send a young boy into battle with a slingshot. It is foolish to march around a city wall for seven days and expect it to fall. It is especially foolish to visit a dead man's grave and invite him to come out. I believe all those foolish stories; do you? If this makes us fools, so be it!

It is not just the cross that provokes people; it's the whole Christian way of life. It is a backwards, flipped upside-down kind of life. Just look at the Beatitudes in Matthew. Right away, Jesus started off by blessing the poor in spirit. The rest of the list reads like personality traits: the mourners, the meek, the peacemakers, the pure in heart, and the merciful. Contrary to what the world may think, being on this list does not make you a loser or a fool. It makes you first in the receiving line for God's greatest blessings.

## On Your Second Birthday
## John 3:1-17, Romans 4:1-5, 13-17

Why do we call the day we are born our date of birth, but that same date every year afterward is called our birthday? Shouldn't they all be anniversaries of our birth? After all, we don't have a wedding day every year! Whatever you choose to call them, our most important birthday is our second. Not when we turn two, but the day when we are born again, our **second birth**day. Our physical birth begins our physical life, which ends with our physical death. Our spiritual rebirth begins our eternal life.

If you think it is hard to grasp the concept of being born again, don't feel too bad. You are not alone. It was a bit of a puzzle for one of the most learned men in Biblical history. Nicodemus knew more about what it took to please God than anyone could possibly accomplish. He also knew that Jesus could only do the things he did with the power of God. The problem that plagued Nicodemus was that by the time the descendants of Abraham became the children of Israel, they were more concerned with the law than they were about pleasing God.

The law that the Jewish leaders loved so much would never get them into God's kingdom. If anything, it would keep them farther away, and would help keep others out, too. Remember when Jesus told the Pharisees that whenever they found a convert they made him twice as fit for hell? There is no salvation in condemnation, no love in the law apart from the saving grace of God. That is why Paul wrote that the descendants of Abraham would not have a chance if the law were the only way.

Our salvation depends on faith. The promise rests on grace, not the law. So we have a reason to celebrate our second birthday. But do we celebrate it? Do we look over the past year and remark at how much we have grown? Not until we know that Christ died for us will we experience our second birthday. The choice has to be made by each person individually. God has no grandchildren. No one comes to faith on the coattails of someone else.

Eventually, Nicodemus must have caught the blowing breeze of the Holy Spirit, or maybe it caught him. He was there at the burial of Jesus, helping to place him in the tomb of Joseph of Arimathea. Had he been around at the time of John and Charles Wesley, I bet I know what his favorite hymn would have been—*Hark the Herald Angels Sing.* The last verse sounds like it was written for him: "Mild he lays his glory by, born that we no more may die, born to raise us from the earth, born to give us second birth."

## A Chance Encounter with Christ
## John 4:4-42, Romans 5:1-11

The title of this sermon is in jest. There are no chance encounters with Christ; opportunities, yes, but never chance. John's gospel gives us a glimpse into the life of one very unlikely evangelist who made quite an impact on her community. She represents the shamed, the down-trodden, and the sinner—all those who were saved by the death and resurrection of Jesus. This was not your typical conversation around the water cooler, but then when is meeting Jesus typical?

Here was a woman with three strikes against her in life, which she would communicate in this conversation. She was, first and foremost, a woman in a culture that considered women to be second-class citizens. She was of that race hated by the Jews, the Samaritans, and she was a source of some degree of scorn, gossip, and criticism among her own people. From their first meeting, she had to know that this would not be an ordinary day. Jesus broke into her preconceived world based on the truth with which she lived.

She was intrigued by what Jesus was offering, but she had to deal with her troubled relationships, past and present. There is always a problem that needs addressing in our lives, some truth that has to come out before we are ready to let Jesus into our lives. When Jesus knew exactly what her life was like, she became a little sidetracked. She saw him as a prophet, and so she began to ask him religious questions. She should have known that a prophet would follow up his questions with some word of judgment from God. Jesus offered none.

This really is an incredible story, but it must reach more than just those residents of Sychar. Whenever we encounter Christ, we should remember this woman who was not afraid to be loved, not afraid to be accepted, warts and all. She knew she did not have to be perfect in order to belong to God. I wonder how many of us know that deep in our hearts.

We all understand about suffering, and although sometimes we wonder why Christians should suffer, we try to focus on what the outcome of suffering—endurance, character, and hope. But who is to say that some of this suffering Paul talked about is not prior to our conversion? The Samaritan woman had her share of suffering, whether it was self-inflicted or at the hands of someone else. Maybe that was where she found the endurance to keep searching for love, the character to avoid those who would judge her, and the hope that the Messiah would one day come.

## The Unsilent Killer
## James 3:5-12

It is a small but powerful muscular object—it enables us to eat and speak and sing. It is undersized in comparison to the other mighty organs that run the body, and it probably ranks least among our health concerns. Yet this little organ can be our undoing. If high blood pressure is the silent killer, then the human tongue is the unsilent killer.

If we were somehow able to keep silent, we might not stay that way for long, because if we repress our emotions, then our other systems go into overdrive. Our blood pressure rises, our breathing becomes quicker, our stomach tightens up, our jaw clenches, and our face flushes, all as a result of the adrenaline coursing through our bloodstream. These physical changes are symptoms of anger. We need to understand where our anger comes from, and how we are expressing it in ways we might not be aware of.

We become angry when our expectations are not met, even if we are not aware of what our expectations are. We are disappointed, we are let down, and we are delayed. Instead of remaining calm or accepting what comes, we get angry, and that anger becomes a motivating force for our tongue.

When we feel this way, we should be alert to the fact that we are at risk of anti-Christian behavior as soon as we open our mouths. We risk showing our dark side, our human side, our sinful side, all because we cannot control that connection between what we feel and what we say. We should pray for God to relieve us of our hurt, our frustration, and our anger. We use expressions like hold your tongue and bite your tongue, but we don't practice what we preach. We say that hopeful little prayer, "From your lips to God's ears. . . ." when we want something good to happen, but silly us, everything travels from our lips to God's ears, blessings and curses from the same mouth.

The one place where we should practice the forgiveness, love, and the compassion that we sing and pray about too often becomes an arena for insincerity and power struggles. A church may be divided by one aisle up the middle or two aisles on the sides, but sometimes it is divided by something else. How would it change our church experience if we were mindful of the fact that in heaven we will see our congregation members every day, not just once a week? Do we really believe that in heaven we will still be able to slight people, speak ill of people, question someone's integrity, or avoid those we do not want to see?

Oh the trouble we get ourselves into from not gaining control over our thoughts and our words. Oh the damage we do by not taking God seriously. There's another expression that we use that I have not mentioned yet, "You took the words right out of my mouth." God wants to take the words right out of our mouths and replace them with kind, loving, compassionate words—words that identify us as Christians to believers and nonbelievers alike.

## Humble Yourself
## James 4:6-10

Remember the little magnetic dogs that kids used to play with? You could make them push against each other, or you could make them stick together. Being in relationship with God is much like playing with magnets. If we draw near to God, God will draw near to us. Unfortunately, we are born with a magnetic pull that draws us toward evil, so our ability to repel the devil and all his tricks can only come from God. We need help to get closer to God and we start by being humble.

James outlines a five-step process to make our relationship with God the best that it can be, the closest that it can be. The first step is to submit ourselves to God. Have you ever tried to play follow the leader with two leaders? You can't very well follow someone without submitting to him or her. Submitting ourselves to God does not mean that we become weak or that we admit that we are defenseless or powerless. It means that we are acknowledging our need for God and trusting in God to protect us.

If we submit to God, then we need to put up resistance to God's enemy, the devil. Resistance should be easy for us, because we can be so stubborn at times. If what we are trying to resist is too tempting, then we run into trouble, and that is one thing the devil excels at, temptation. There is a word about temptation in our Lord's Prayer, but we need to remember the strength of temptation when our eyes are open, between times of prayer.

We also need to avoid being stained by the sins of the world. We do this by asking God to cleanse us on the inside, within our hearts. Once we are clean, we have to maintain our spiritual hygiene. Through prayer and the word of God, we can cover ourselves with something like an antibacterial protection against the bacteria of sin infesting the world.

We do need more than just protection, however. We also need a clean slate, a wiping away of our sins through confession and forgiveness. Recount your sins when you pray. Try to recall every unkind word, every selfish behavior. You know when you're guilty, because you feel that little twinge of remorse. Why not admit to God and to yourself that there is still work to be done in your life?

The last step in this process is to humble ourselves before God and watch as we are built up. God will show us what we can become and what our obedience is worth gradually, as we learn to trust more and more. Prayer is a key factor in all of these steps, because if we are ever in doubt as to how to be submissive or how to resist temptation—even how to repent—we can talk to God about it and our eyes will be opened. Bear in mind that this process is ongoing and constant. We must start again every day by surrendering to God, keeping ourselves safe from sin, living a pure and holy life, recognizing when we have done wrong, and never giving ourselves more credit than we deserve.

## Patience Takes Time
## James 5:7-12

Oh how we hate to wait! The trouble with patience is, we can only learn it by waiting. We only gain patience by keeping it. Like it or not, patience is a necessary part of life, especially in the modern world where, despite technology, it seems we wait for everything. The line we are in will always be slower than the other. The package we need for a special occasion will always arrive the day after. We have many opportunities to learn patience.

James added a special situation where patience comes in handy, and showed us why waiting is so important. James said we do not so much learn patience as we allow it to happen. Patience is a product of our suffering, but we do not like to hear that. We already think that every wait makes us suffer enough. Sometimes it is better to suffer and wait than to hurry and suffer for entirely different reasons.

There is one event that we might hasten to see, and that is the return of Christ. Over the centuries, there has been speculation and calculation as to when that might occur, all to no avail. Scripture tells us that Christ does not even know the hour. All we can do is wait and be ready. James told us to wait patiently, like the farmer who prepares the ground, plants the seeds, tends the crops, and then, having done all under his control, he watches the skies and waits for the rain.

A farmer's life is often uncertain and is definitely a waiting game. James cited other great figures who excelled at waiting: the prophets of old, who spoke faithfully the words God gave them and then waited expectantly for the people to respond; and Job, who literally sat and waited for some explanation of what was going on in his life.

James urged us to strengthen our hearts in order to help us wait. To have a strong heart is to be resolute, full of courage, and committed to the end. The most important detail for the Christian is to remember that our suffering is temporary. Christ is coming, and when that day comes, all suffering will cease. Although millions have died before Christ's return, the day is coming.

Impatience does more than frustrate us; it often leads us into temptation. It may be tempting to take over the reins of a situation, or to take matters into our own hands when we are waiting for an answer to prayer. Often we end up even more frustrated and angry than if we had been a little more patient. We grumble because we can't see the larger picture of our lives.

Looking ahead can help us a great deal. We will realize that in the end, all those little frustrations and delays will not mean a thing in comparison to eternity with God. Look ahead to the outcome God has promised for our lives. God is compassionate and merciful. All our wrongs will be made right, but in God's time. All our waiting will be made worthwhile.

## Forgiving the Unforgivable
## John 13:21-32

To be human is to be in community, and to be in community is to be at risk. We are at the mercy of the behavior and choices of others, but our response is up to us. Deciding whether or not to forgive after someone has wronged us is often a difficult choice. What would our lives be like if we knew where and when those times would come? Could we forgive if we knew beforehand how much we would be hurt? I would venture to say that none of us would willingly accept pain unless it was to spare someone we love.

Parents understand the risk of being hurt simply by loving someone, but sometimes people without children cannot understand their choices. If you are not personally invested in a situation, you cannot always see the outcome. Jesus predicted his death at least three times. The disciples were present, and once Peter even protested, but they chose not to listen. To them it was admitting defeat because they did not understand the outcome. In their minds they were not personally invested in the situation yet.

Judas was listening. He was personally invested. He had a motivation to betray Jesus. The announcement of the betrayal caused the disciples to be distressed, but they still were not 100% invested. Their first concern was who the betrayer would be. Jesus, in effect, offered Judas a chance to back out. By taking the bread, Judas sealed his fate and allowed Satan in. This was more than just a human drama; this was a battle between good and evil. And still the disciples had no idea.

We are simply not as capable of forgiveness as Jesus was. It breaks our hearts to think of him bloodied and beaten, broken and bruised, betrayed and buried. We cry with him in the garden, but do we forgive with him at the cross? Anger can be a very effective tool if it is tempered by righteousness, but most of the time it just becomes an accessory. Some people never leave home without it.

Whenever you pray to God, asking for your daily bread, bear in mind the request that you make next—asking for forgiveness while promising to be forgiving. If we are bold enough to remind God that we need bread every day of our lives, then we should be humble enough to be reminded that we need to offer and accept forgiveness every day of our lives. Pain and betrayal are a very real part of life. Being unforgiving is a part of death, the death of the image that God so desperately wants to create in each of us.

## Moving in the Right Direction
## John 14:1-14

Do all roads lead to heaven? The answer is a resounding no! Not all the people of the world on a spiritual journey are even interested in going to heaven. Some are only looking for inner peace or harmony, some only want happiness right here on earth. So no, all roads do not lead to heaven because not all roads are looking for Jesus. But for those who are looking for Jesus, there is only one way—through Jesus himself.

Jesus alone stands as the entrance into God's kingdom. Make no mistake: He is not standing at the gates of heaven like a bouncer, behind a velvet rope, checking his exclusive list, sending more people away than he is letting in. His statement that he is the way did not mean that only he decides who will enter heaven; it meant that he is the only access. Trying to sneak in on good behavior or through exorbitant gifts to charity or by meditating or pilgrimage or rituals or sacrifice will not work. Only through accepting the work of Christ on the cross can we get to heaven.

These claims that Jesus made in John's gospel may sound narrow, intolerant, and exclusive, but they are true. Jesus is not the way because he can show us the way; he is the way. He is the way in which God expressed enormous love for us, and he is the way for us to reach God. He is the only route, the only gate, the only access to heaven. To get there we must follow him.

Jesus is the truth because he shows us the reality of God and the nature of God, which is loving, holy, and just. Other religions have multiple gods. Even man is a god in some belief systems, but there is only one God and we have knowledge of our God through our knowledge of Jesus. Jesus is the life because he overcame death and spared us from being eternally separated from God.

Our eternal life is unearned and free. We do not work for it because we cannot. We cannot believe we are good enough because we never will be. But Jesus has paid the price for us and we are forgiven, and that we can believe. We must go in the direction Jesus leads us if we want heaven to be our home, because he has shown us through his life and death that his words are true. He came from heaven and he returned to heaven. He alone knows the way.

## Comfort Measures
## John 14:15-21

Is it wrong for us to seek comfort in other people when they can be so awful to us? Better that than to seek comfort in too much food or too much alcohol or too much shopping. But the comfort that the world offers us, even through those we love, can never match what God offers to us. Because we have the benefit of Jesus coming to earth for the very specific purpose of saving us, we also now have the benefit of a companion through life who will never leave us. In a world where promises are often untrue, we have a word that we can always trust.

This word came straight from the Word made flesh, Jesus. On the night before Jesus died for the sake of the world, Jesus turned his thoughts to the disciples' anxiety. He said a great many things to them in those last hours. It would be hard to say what they actually remembered. But those overwhelmed disciples did eventually remember the promise made to them. The comforter came.

The nature of this comforter, the Holy Spirit, is the Spirit's unique role in our spiritual lives as a guide. What makes the Spirit so incredibly vital to our faith is that the Holy Spirit shares so many similarities with the earthly person of Jesus. Jesus was God's gift to the world, sent for the sake of God's people. God sent the Holy Spirit as a gift. Jesus came to act as a counselor and guide. Now the Holy Spirit does that work in Jesus' place.

For us, the Holy Spirit is equal to God and Jesus in both power and authority. Each of these three has a vital link to us as individuals and as a community. This is the most special relationship that we have. Yet we fail to live out its fullness because it is difficult for us to comprehend that we actually have not only the ear of the creator of the universe whenever we want it, but also the power and the love of God living within us. If we really believed how incredibly blessed we are, we would not be able to believe it!

When we think of comfort measures, we think of a mother's kiss, a friendly hug, or a soothing bath. We comfort the sick, we comfort the dying, we comfort the grieving, but eventually our comfort runs out. Not so with the Spirit of God. The Spirit's comfort is with us always.

## Empty Tomb Vs. Open Grave
## John 11:1-4, 38-44

An empty tomb. An open grave. One signifies a victory over death, the other stands waiting for an occupant. Both are a resting place for the dead, the final chapter in the mortal life. So why do we rejoice at the thought of one and weep at the thought of the other? Two reasons, really: knowledge and perspective. Without the knowledge of the power of God, one's perspective of death may be devoid of all hope.

Death leaves a terrible stench in what God had created to be a perfect world. The smell of death has followed the human race around ever since Adam dropped a piece of forbidden fruit on the lush ground of Paradise. It is a smell that brings tears to your eyes, and weep we must, because to suppress our tears would be to suppress our human nature.

Jesus wept, did he not? He stood among the mourners before the tomb of Lazarus and wept for the sad situation facing the family and friends. He wept with them, and he wept for them. He weeps with us, and he weeps for us. Christ's tears give us permission to shed our own. So grieve, but do not grieve like those who do not know the rest of the story, like those without knowledge. With knowledge of Christ, the rest of the story is a happy ending.

Even when the ending is happy the waiting can be unbearable. Life is definitely a waiting game. Those at the end of life would sooner see the day of their deliverance than to wait in pain or loneliness. The Psalms speak of the agony of waiting, "How long, O Lord?" In the story of Lazarus, the answer was four days. Four days elapsed from the beginning of the story to the end. Four days a man lay dead in a tomb, waiting for life.

You would not send for a healer once the undertaker had done his or her job. But if the healer is Jesus, there is nothing that can crush the hopes of the most doubtful mourner. An empty tomb or an open grave? It all depends on your perspective, and the one who can change your perspective is the one who took your place in death.

## Teach Your Children Well
## Psalm 78, Deuteronomy 11

Child development and psychology experts have theories of basic human needs. The simplest needs are for food, sleep, etc. Next are the needs for safety and shelter. Then there is the need for love, and finally the need for good self-esteem. If all these needs are met, you should become a pretty happy and healthy individual. Where would we place the need for faith in our development?

If we strive to be truly balanced people, then we need to place our need for God very high. The author of this psalm had a purpose for retelling the story of what God had done for Israel. He started by reminding people of God's blessing, and then he moved on to what their appropriate response should be. He said that the faith of future generations rested in the hands of those who came before. What an outstanding responsibility!

This psalmist must have had Deuteronomy 11 in mind, for there we find God's instructions to teach the next generations. We have numerous public service ads encouraging parents to talk to their children about smoking or drinking or drugs. Why are there no messages about the importance of talking to our kids about faith? The lesson of Deuteronomy 11 is to continually speak about God, whether at home or away. From this children will learn not to change their behavior or their values in different situations.

Keeping families connected in faith for as long as possible helps to ensure that the story will not be lost, so that God's blessings will continue as long as the heavens are above the earth. That is a very long time! Whatever we pass on to our children or grandchildren, it must be worthy of God and filled with sincerity and truth, not merely empty practice. Children need a defense against the doubt and apathy of a culture that sees no benefit in faith.

What would you like to hand down to your descendants? Will you give them a hope for the future and hearts that are steadfast? Will you tell them that they are children of God and that the story of Israel is still being told today?

## What Dancing Can Lead To
## 2 Samuel 6:1-5, 12-19; Mark 6:14-29

It is a problem that has plagued society for ages, a source of conflict between children and parents. Young people want to dance and concerned parents want to keep them as far apart as possible because of what parents fear could result from dancing. Still, as long as there have been concerned parents, dancing has been a national craze. The dances change as the music changes, and the kids keep on dancing.

Our scripture readings feature two dancing stories. Both stories involve a man and a woman, which only makes sense for dancing, but these were not dance partners, and these are not typical stories of couples dancing together. They featured men who were concerned about keeping up appearances while trying to maintain their faith. The women involved were not all that interested in proper religious practices.

The moral of the story lies in why the dancers dances and whom they were dancing for. King David was the first dancer. He became carried away with the excitement of bringing the Ark of the Covenant back to Jerusalem. He was dancing for joy, in just his undergarments. It is clear that his wife Michal was not pleased. She lost whatever respect she may have had for David when she saw him prancing around in his underwear, his conduct unbecoming a king.

Our second dance number was different from David's story. It also involved a husband and wife, but this time the dancer was a woman dragged into a murderous plot. The man was also a king, Herod Antipas. He shared one trait with King David: he had stolen the wife of another man. John the Baptist publicly denounced this affair, and for that reason he had been imprisoned by Herod.

No one really knows how long John would have remained in prison had it not been for the intervention of Herodias.

She enlisted the help of her daughter Salome in a dance that would lead to the death of John. This seductive dance was certainly conduct unbecoming a princess. Weakness and failure seem to be prevalent themes among the royal figures of the Bible, but they are just as easy to find among the common people. Sin will find a willing participant in any walk of life.

Dancing with the wrong partner can make men and women do things they later regret. People who dance with the devil are headed for disaster. There may be times in our lives when we find ourselves engaged in some dance or another. It is not necessarily a dance of our own choosing, but we dance all the same. This dancing may lead us farther away from God.

The danger from all this dancing is that we may rely too much on our own ability. There is only one person we ever need for a partner. He has tangoed with temptation, waltzed with worry, and danced with death. He knows the steps and will never step on our toes. The only thing we have to do is take his hand and let him lead.

## The Illusion of Brotherly Love
## Luke 15:1-2, 11-32

There was a man who had two sons. This could be the beginning of so many stories from Scripture, and it would be hard to decide to which father and sons Jesus referred. Could it be Adam, whose sons were a murderer and his victim? Could it be Eli, whose sons were more of a curse than a blessing? Could it be the unknown John, whose sons became two of the most trusted disciples, or Zebedee, whose sons would argue over which of them was the greatest?

This man and his sons are without names. What we know of them we learn from their personalities and their behaviors. Their story was short, yet revealing. Whether or not you find yourself taking sides may depend on how well you can relate to the story. Imagine you are the father, and your younger son comes to you one day to ask something from you that goes against all tradition, all sense of what is right and proper. Do you give him whatever he wants in order to make him happy, or do you try to save face and do what is right?

For the younger son to want his freedom to go out and see the world was not unusual, but for him to ask for what should have come to him only on his father's death was shameful. It put both the father and the elder son in an awkward position. The young man lost so much along the way: his home, his family, the respect of his friends, and his dignity. The father's life was also filled with loss. He lost a portion of his wealth, and he lost a great deal of credibility in the eyes of his older son.

I think it was the older brother who lost the most in the family. He lost the companionship of his younger brother and his sense of compassion and understanding. He was burdened by a sense of duty to his father and a sense of perpetual resentment. An angry heart is a terrific breeding ground for sin and hate.

The saddest part of this parable is how much these three men misunderstood each other, when they really had a great deal in common. It is interesting what the brothers had in common. Both looked to other people to help them out. When the younger son was starving and wanted to eat the pigs' leftovers, no one gave him anything. When the older one was back at home patiently serving his father, he was never given an animal for a feast. Because those who are lost do not think they are deserving of anything, they do not ask.

Jesus used this parable to illustrate the illusion of brotherly love that existed between the people he came to save and the religious leaders who wanted nothing to do with them. There has always been a certain amount of division within the family of God, just as there was a division in the father's house. This division comes from forgetting what is important: not status or rank, but belonging.

## Who Are You Wearing?
## Colossians 3:12-17

It is funny how award shows have gone from a focus on talent to a focus on fashion. Now, instead of asking the celebrities what they will say if they should win, the hosts ask, "Who are you wearing?" We might not live in that kind of high society with designer clothing, but we can still ask that question in regard to our faith. Paul said that we should be clothed in a special garment, not visible to the eye, but detectable all the same.

It is a special garment because it is modeled after the one worn by someone very special to us whose style we should all try to copy. We who have chosen to follow Christ are instructed to make for ourselves a garment fashioned after the one worn by Christ. We need to clothe ourselves with compassion, kindness, humility, gentleness, patience, for-giveness, and bind all those together with love.

We are also to let the peace of Christ rule in our hearts. This requires us to make a conscious choice. We have to let peace rule in our hearts. It will not just come to us if we are still ruled by other factors and emotions that cloud our thinking and actions. In the culture of the ancient Near East, the heart was believed to be the center of emotional thought. If we are to be successful in letting peace gain control over our hearts, then our next step is to be thankful, which would seem to be a natural reaction to being at peace.

Next, Paul said that we are to continue in our self-improvement program by letting the word of God dwell within us. It should richly dwell through scripture and songs and words of encouragement to others. Notice that the way we appear on the outside begins to change how we appear on the inside. It is all part of the idea that clothes make the person. Our goal is to have the presence of Christ so much a part of us that whatever we do or say is done in his name in a way that makes us thankful to him.

Every few years we have to sort through our closets and remove those things that just do not fit us or suit us anymore. It is the only way to make room for all the new things we need now that we have changed. The same is true when heeding Paul's wisdom. In order to make room for what we need to make us feel better and look better and become better, we need to rid ourselves of what we do not need, what does not suit us, what keeps us enslaved to last year's trends.

Let us sweep out the cobwebs of our former selves that remain within us. Let us replace the negative emotions lurking in our hearts with the overwhelming peace of Christ. Let us make the word of God a priority in our days until our demeanor, our attitude, and our very speech reflects the presence of God in our lives. Let us weave for ourselves a beautiful garment that only our eyes can see, but the whole world cannot help but notice. Let us make a new fashion statement so that everyone will be asking, "Who are you wearing? " and we can honestly reply, "I am wearing the image of my creator."

# Closings

Perhaps no element of worship is as important as the end. This is certainly true of the sermon, which must conclude in a way that brings the whole message down to a single thought. The close of worship should be a reminder of all that has transpired, all that was sung and spoken in prayer and in praise. It should leave us with the true feeling of amen—so be it.

When we think of the close of worship, we generally think of a final hymn and a benediction, followed by some type of musical response. Whether we chose a benediction to be read in unison by the congregation, or perhaps a dismissal given by the worship leader, the words that we say at the end of our worship should have an influence on us. May these examples of closing words give that influence you seek.

# Benedictions

## 1

We are built together as the body of Christ, each of us with our own special gifts and graces to complete the work of God. How can we show our spirit of community to the world without showing it first to one another?

## 2

Living in community was never meant to be easy, but it was meant to be Christian. Amen.

## 3

We have been called by God to show love to the world. We have eaten at God's table and received God's grace. May we always make the connection between these truths. Amen.

## 4

God has shown us how to be humble. Will we now take up that challenge and show God that we have been paying attention?

## 5

Whatever we are willing to give, the Lord is willing to bless. Let our love for Christ be reflected in our prayers, our presence, our gifts, and our service. Amen.

## 6

God has placed in our lives many, many examples of faith. Some we have met, some we have not. Some of them will be here long after we are gone. We need to live in the promise of God's faithful people. Amen.

## 7

May the Lord grant you peace through your knowledge of the Lord until we are together again in the Lord's house. Amen.

## 8

Will we share what we have been given—God's promise, God's love, and God's truth—with others? If we keep it to ourselves, we are failing to uphold our calling. Amen.

WORSHIP PLANNING GUIDEBOOK

## 9

Now we see only dimly, but soon we will see with the clarity of God. Until that time, then, let us show our willingness to be guided through life. Amen.

## 10

Our God has told us how we are to live and whom we are to love. Let everything we do become a religious observance of God's grace. Amen.

## 12

God's love remains an eternal mystery to us, one that we are not meant to understand. Yet God asks us to share that love with others. Amen.

## 13

Jesus told us to go into all the world and make disciples. Our first responsibility to Christ is to be disciples. Amen.

## 14

We have been a part of something much bigger than ourselves. We have worshiped the creator of the world. What greater privilege could we have after this?

## 15

Worship brings us together as family, but what keeps us together is our mutual love of God. Amen.

## 16

Singing, praying, and worship bring meaning to life as we spend time in God's house. What can we do to bring that same meaning to life everywhere else?

## 17

Whether we are shouting or whispering, praying or praising, God is waiting to hear what we have to say. Amen.

## 18

Being in God's presence does not end when we walk through the sanctuary door. God goes with us into the world and guides our every step. Amen.

## 19

May God, who will bring all things to completion, complete that great work that was begun within all of us. Amen.

## 20

Because God first loved us, we are called to love others. May we first be able to love ourselves and believe that we are worthy of love. Amen.

# Dismissals

## 1

People of God, rejoice! You are going out to meet the world as representatives of Christ. God has entrusted this great responsibility to those who love the Lord.

## 2

God's great amen is what gives us power and faith to live in a world that rejects God's son. Go now and show your belief to the world.

## 3

Because we are loved, we are able to show love in return. Because we are forgiven, we are enabled to forgive. We also live because Christ lives! Amen.

## 4

Where God's people combine, there God is in our midst. We are here because we are called to be. What we share of ourselves is an extension of God. Amen.

## 5

Life is change, it is conflict, and it is work. Life in Christ is never meant to be perfect, yet Christians must always work at being perfected.

## 6

May you leave this house of worship a kinder, more loving people because you are taking with you the enormous gift of God's love.

## 7

Go in peace, into a world longing to hear the message of the gospel. Let others see the good news alive in you.

## 8

We do not leave worship behind when our church service is over. We take our worship with us so that everyone can share our love of God.

## 9

Have you been touched? Have you been challenged? If you have it is time for you to go beyond this moment and use those feelings to change your world.

## 10

Fear not! Goodness and mercy are ready to follow you when you make your way out of the sanctuary and into the world.

# The Invitation

We now have covered all the components of worship that facilitate the expression of our feelings about God. However, our participation in worship must elicit from us a response of some kind, whether that be a hymn or a litany or perhaps the service of Holy Communion. Another form of response is aimed at those worshipers who may not have made a commitment to Christ. In that respect, from beginning to end the worship service should be building to a decision.

While the object of worship is to praise God, that should include the kind of praise that serves as an evangelistic tool. Not everyone seated in the pews is at the same level of faith as those seated around them. The response a person makes to the message may be one of first-time commitment to Christ.

The invitation must be given in a way that is non-threatening and does not cause those to whom it is directed to feel that they are the objects of unwanted attention. Be mindful of what emotions the worship service and particularly the message may have evoked in the individual. They may be feeling guilty, or lost, or desperate, or even relieved. Make the words of the invitation welcoming and reflective of God's grace. This is a momentous decision that we are privileged to set in motion.

The following is an example of how an invitation may be worded. It may follow immediately after the sermon as a lead in to prayer, or it may take place after the singing of the final hymn. In either case, there should be provisions made to accommodate those who may wish to pray at the altar rail. Here is one example:

If there is anyone here today who has heard God's call or felt God's touch for the first time, I would ask for your special attention. Maybe you have never accepted Christ's sacrifice made for you. Maybe you've never believed in that gift before today. It could be that something said here today has opened your eyes to see how much God loves you. God wants you as a part of the kingdom of heaven. What you need to do is simple, yet profound. You need to acknowledge that you are a sinner, believe that Christ died to save you from sin, confess that Jesus is your Lord, and invite him into your heart.

Another circumstance may involve persons who have some knowledge of the Christian way, who may have once believed, but have become misled or drawn apart from God. In that case, the invitation may be more along this line:

Is there someone here today whose heart has been moved by God? Maybe you have found yourself wondering why God seems far away, or perhaps you have been doing your best to avoid God. You know what the Lord requires of you, but maybe you don't know where to start. Don't feel hopeless: You are not so far from God that you cannot come back. Repeat the words of this prayer and be reminded of how much God loves you, of how much you love God.

The prayer would then go something like this:

Dear God, I am coming to you for forgiveness of my sins. I have no need to list what I have done, for you know. I release my sins to you, and I ask that you fill my dark heart with your presence and your love. Show me the direction you have for my life and keep me close to you. Thank you for your loving son and the sacrifice that spared my life. You are my joy and my future. Amen.

Bear in mind that these invitations are only samples of what you may use. You can gauge the needs and the openness of your listeners by trusting God to give you that insight. God will also give you the words to say, and therefore you should make your invitation impromptu and avoid reading a prepared statement.

# Putting It All Together

So we have all the components of worship chosen, and we know what we want to say. How do we put it all together in a way that best expresses our choices? Using our basic pattern of worship helps us to understand the focus areas of our worship, and having a theme or purpose keeps us on track. The rest of the service, such as music or a children's message, should complement the other components that are based primarily on the scripture or a topic.

Hymns may be chosen to reflect a scripture passage or overall theme of the service. Attention should be paid to the way the hymns accompany each other and help to convey the feeling intended in the worship. Seasonal music should also aid in the spirit of the service, yet we do not need to solely rely on Advent, Christmas, Lenten or Easter hymns in our Advent, Christmas, Lenten, or Easter worship.

Other hymns can be utilized to reinforce or communicate messages of grace, salvation, redemption, love, etc. There is often a great, untapped well of theology to be found in the hymns we sing, and with the proper preparation and planning, these verses may make a major impact in the worship experience that may well rival the sermon.

The following pages are for your worship planning use. View one is designed to help you sketch out the various components of the service by category. View two is designed to allow you space to put it all together in a bulletin format. Blank outline planning sheets have also been included for your use. Remember that you can pick and choose which worship components you will use, and you may tailor the service according to your needs and preferences.

The key to planning worship in which everything falls into place is consistency and continuity of the basis of the worship service. Choose your text and message and then have fun building up the worship with music and liturgies and prayers to accent and highlight that message. Good luck and God bless!

# View One Planning Sheet

## Entrance

**Gathering:** This is the time for greeting each other, reading announcements, and for prelude music.

**Greeting and hymn:** A welcome is extended to the worshipers and a selection of music is used to set the tone.

This is where the **Call to Worship** or the **Opening Sentences** would be used.

**Opening prayers and praise:** This could be an **Invocation** or a **Prayer of Confession**, or a **Unison Prayer**.

In the place of a Psalter, a litany may be used.

## Proclamation and Response

**A Prayer for Illumination** may be led by the worship leader prior to the reading of scripture.

**Scripture:** Selected texts from the Old Testament, Gospels, and Epistles may be read.

**Sermon:** The message is brought to the people.

**Response to the Word:** This may take the form of an invitation to commitment, or on special occasions may include a baptism, confirmation, or receiving of members.

A litany or other responsive reading could also be utilized here.

**Concerns and Prayers:** At this time, joys and concerns, the pastoral prayer, and the Lord's Prayer would be featured.

**Confession, Pardon, and Peace:** If a confessional or congregational prayer was not done earlier, this is the correct time for those worship features.

This is also the appropriate time for passing of the peace among the worshipers.

**Offering:** This is generally followed by a **Prayer of Dedication**, a doxology, or possibly a hymn.

## Thanksgiving

If no communion is planned, then the prayer of dedication may actually serve as a prayer of thanksgiving, or another prayer may be substituted.

**Sending Forth**

**Hymn or song:** The congregational hymn may precede the **Dismissal** or the **Benediction**.

**Going Forth:** A brief hymn or chorus of response may follow, or the postlude may be played while the congregation leaves the worship service.

The individual preferences of the worship planner or congregation may no follow the flow of the basic pattern of worship exactly as this sample page indicates. For example, in the worship service I conduct each week, the congregational and pastoral prayers come before the reading of Scripture, and the offering is taken before the sermon. The order of the worship components within the pattern is not as crucial as is the intention with which they are chosen and placed.

# View Two Planning Sheet

## Entrance

The various headings used for this section include Gathering, Prepare for Worship, and Gathering to Worship the Lord.

At prayer time, the headings may include Time of Prayer and Reflection or Community Called to Prayer.

## Proclamation and Response

Prior to the reading of scripture and the sermon, a title such as Proclaim the Word or **Proclamation of the Word** may appear.

The taking of offering may be entitled **We Bring Our Gifts** or **Offerings from All**.

## Thanksgiving

As the third component, thanksgiving primarily involves the service of Communion, it may not have a separate heading to mark the transition from proclamation and response.

## Sending Forth

Here the division headings may include **Go and Serve** or **Go Forth to Serve**.

# Worship Planning Sheet

## Entrance

Gathering

Greeting and Hymn

Opening Prayers and Praise

## Proclamation and Response

Prayer for Illumination

Scripture

Sermon

Response to the Word

Concerns and Prayers

Confession, Pardon, and Peace

Offering

## Thanksgiving

## Sending Forth

Hymn or Song

Dismissal or Benediction

Going Forth